PAINTING WITH WORDS

A catalogue record for this book is available from the National Library of Australia

Published 2021

ISBN: 978-0-6453437-0-0 (epub)
ISBN: 978-0-6453006-9-7 (paperback)
ISBN: 978-0-6453437-1-7 (PDF)

9 780645 300697

Published with the aid of Jumble Books and
    Publishers
(jumblebooksandpublishers.com)

Image credit:

Painting with Words

Landscapes in Verse

by

Richard Greene

Richard Greene is a poet, or has been at least since he retired from a 38-year career in international development. A lawyer by training, he fell into his development career by accident when, after law school, though planning not to practice law but interested in international affairs, he accepted an unsolicited job offer from the U.S. Agency for International Development. After a few years in Washington (or Foggy Bottom, as the location of the U.S. foreign policy establishment is known), he was assigned as legal advisor to the USAID mission in Laos and there discovered that the development business suited his interests and inclinations very well.

Greene wrote poetry beginning in the 8th grade and continued through college where he studied with a Professor, Henry Rago, who later became editor of *Poetry* magazine, the leading U.S. poetry journal. However, he wrote few poems after law school as he became absorbed in international development, but turned back to poetry as he neared retirement.

Contents

Painting with Words

Words are my medium.
I paint with them,
clumps of words,
tincture of words,
acrylic, tempera, fresco,
bright colored words,
words insistently monochromatic,
words full of light
or shadow,
words airy as clouds,
heavy as iron,
living words,
inanimate words,
words sumptuous and simple,
realist
expressionist
surrealist
impressionist
I lay my words on with gusto.

Geneva Dawn

Smoke balances
on the chimney pots
like kelp
undulating
in the stillness.
Below the bridge
silver fish flash
through the gilded reflection
of Mont Blanc,
a cache
of sunken treasure.

Andean Scenes

snowy peaks
reverberating above the thunder,
Tungurahua
Chimborazo
Sangay

eucalyptus forests cascading
down green slopes,
exuding their cool incense,
narrow leaves shimmering
in the rarefied light

haciendas luxuriating
in the valleys
while the patchwork farms
of the dispossessed
cling to impossible slopes

Marblehead

Sun spangled
sail flecked
homespun bay,
cloud bannered
beach blazoned,
yes wine dark too,

a fanfare of trumpets
and cellos,
the somber brilliance
of a northern sea

To the Source

I've lived near the river's end,
where its wide waters slide
into bay and ocean,
and watched ships ride the deep water.
Often I've dreamed
of tracing it to its source
past the farthest reach of ocean vessels,
past stretches where the silken flow
is trimmed with frothy white
and you can see the mountains' bones
beneath the water,
climbing, ever climbing
through field and forest
at last to the place,
in a watery meadow perhaps
or hidden under trees,
where the great river is born,
issuing from the earth
in a stream so small
you could cup it in your hands.

Titicaca

the lake
astonishingly blue
in the mouth of nevados
that poke like teeth
through the dry land

a creature in whose throat
one sees the cosmos

Eclipse

Leaves glow
against a darkening sky,
like amber
the ebbing light flows
over fields and trees,
a vast shadow fills the air,
stars pierce the unfinished day
and Earth seems to age
under its swollen moon.

The Housatonic Near Kent

Slowly
the river unwinds
through flat fields,
scarcely stirring the reeds,
its voice not even a murmur.

Fish hang
in the hushed flow
weightless as shadows.

What if Eden

were not in biblical lands
but in Africa's fecund matrix
where herds of zebra
flash across the savanna
and giraffes overtop the trees;
in the Great Rift, for instance,
wide enough for Noah's flood
between its high rims;

near sea-deep Lake Malawi
where towering mesas
hide whole shires
atop their capacious crowns;

amidst the massive flowers
of the Ruwenzori;

hidden in the rain forests of the Congo
where great-trunked trees
cast a spell of perpetual twilight;

under the spray of a cataract
at the center of the continent
where I found a tiny tree frog
glistening green
in the trumpet of a lily-like fungus,
as if newly created there;

or up-country in Guinea
where waterfalls dangle
from the edges of jungle-clad cliffs,
like remnants of a bygone world.

The Lake at Evening

The sky is still,
the water too,
hushed,
expectant,
as the worldlight dims
and trees silhouette
a watery stage
where fish dimple
the plainsong surface
and birds pirouette
through the gilded air.

Landscape in Gray

Beneath the leafless trees,
their branches etched on fog,
the river spreads,
metallic in its cold repose.

One of Those Rare Moments

It was one of those rare moments
when the Earth holds its breath,
the air is utterly still
and lakes are transformed into mirrors
reflecting sky and trees
with serene precision.

Once in the Andes

I came upon a village
high on the altiplano
barely below the perpetual snow
a place so cold
no crops grow there
and only the native fauna are able
to browse the moss-low grass,
withstand the ethereal chill.
There impassive alpacas graze,
and guanacos
shy of men
course over the high land
with stiff, swift strides.

So the villagers,
heirs of a once proud empire
(architects of the portal at Tiahuanaco
opening now only on the sky),
live with these creatures
in long kinship,
weaving coarse cloth from their wool,
shaping footwear from their hides,
feeding of their flesh,
trekking for days
to trade their meat and cloth and leather
down past the snowy ramparts of the cordillera
down through the clouds.

On the village square
I heard them intone their ancient music,
the rasp of their flutes
like the wail of the Andean wind.

There's Something About a Lake

the mysteries
beneath its surface;
its alien inhabitants
in their alien world;
its changing moods and attire,
vivacious blue,
tranquil green,
somber gray;
garments plain
or ornamented
with wind whipped lace
or sequins of sunlight;
calm as a monk in meditation,
contorted with stormy anger,
or performing its glad dance
under a sunny sky.

There's something about a lake
that plays on our hearts and minds.

Seeing Water

Even now, in my sixty-eighth year,
I still experience a thrill
when rounding a curve
or topping a hill
I come upon a body of water,
whether festive blue
or sullen gray,
open to view
or half hidden by trees.
Even a small lake
I pass almost every day
still surprises me
with a pulse of pleasure.
It summons up, I suppose,
the lake where I spent
my childhood summers,
its mile-wide waters
abloom with sails,
where I fished
as day segued into night
and gold streaked
the sky's book of hours,

the remote Canadian lakes
where I basked in a solitude
broken only by the lonely cry of loons,
moose grazing in the shallows
or the occasional band of Cree
in their quiet canoes,
gathering wild rice,
and overhead at night
the sky-spanning, pulsating
polychrome curtain
of the aurora,

or the Hudson
where I whiled away my time
watching ships slide languorously by,
the slow kaleidoscope
of clouds and sky
over the Jersey bank,
or seagulls
gliding against the towering Palisades
so steady on their wings
the world seemed to move
while they stood still,
and in the background always
the tremendous harp of the bridge
gracing the river's canyon
as it might the very gates of heaven.

Then there's the Pacific
which, more precocious than Balboa,
I first saw at age six,
having come from the east
with my grandmother
who, indulging me,
drove straight to the water,
not even stopping
at our new home.
It was overcast that day
and I was disappointed
that the great ocean
wasn't the least bit blue.
Still, it was the Pacific,
spreading all the way
from California to Cathay
with a leap
only the imagination could equal.

Cotapaxi

Just below a great snowy cone in the Andes
on a broad, flat shelf of mountain
wild horses race
keeping pace
with wind-driven clouds overhead,
breath steaming
long manes swirling,
exhilarated,
as if created
just moments before
out of the primordial chaos.

Flurries

Snowflakes falling
when I step out of the house
remind me of cherry blossom petals
swirling in a spring wind in Kyoto,
of a cloud of yellow butterflies
in the Amazonian lowlands of Bolivia,
of the joyously colored fish
on the reefs off a Caribbean coast,
of a great flock
of very pink flamingos
in the Galapagos,
of crowds of color and light
that transmute
even the planet's most prosaic sites.

The Icehouse

When I was a boy
there was an icehouse
in the place where we spent our summers.
Crews quarried ice in winter
from a nearby lake
and buried it in sawdust.
With the warm weather
men in leather aprons came
on trucks loaded with the big cold blocks
which they hefted into our ice chest
with outsize tongs.

I liked to visit the icehouse
for its mountain coolness
in the heat of summer
and the wonder of the ice
preserved like ancient glaciers.

The icehouse is gone now
and the men in leather aprons
and the time when I could make believe
there were mountains and glaciers
in an old wooden shed.

The View from Berkeley

Fog awakens
to a rising sun
on a sheet of shale green bay,
stretches,
uncovering the comely shoulders
of Mount Tamalpais,
slides down
the taut tendons of the bridge,
but leaves the city's towers
still half veiled,
as it slowly, slowly rises
from its bed.

Orinocos of the Imagination

I've never been to the Orinoco
and have seen few photos of it,
but I feel I know its sinuous lengths,
winding between thick jungle walls,
flashing silver in the sun,
delicate waterfalls
threading from cloud-shrouded cliffs,
dense foliage
adorned with birds of kindergarten colors
and jaguars that merge into shadow,
the insistent music
of bird cry and monkey chatter,
dugouts and caimans
scoring its sleek waters,
those who people its valley
gliding nearly naked
through twilight forests,
dappled by the distant sun.
I know these lush landscapes
from my dreams.

Soundscape, East River

The spiked cries of gulls echo
among the mute towers of Manhattan.
The thrum of ships' engines hums
over the polished water.
The city's pulse resonates
in the great string chamber
of the bridge.

Surrounded by the Universe

In these early morning hours
in this room
it begins
stretching outward
from the circle of lamplight on my desk
to the leaf-dappled streetlight across the way
to the moon's chalky mirror
to the distant incandescence of the stars,
from the scratch of my pen
to the scrapings of insects in surrounding fields
to the faint but ceaseless aura of traffic sounds
through the intermittent silences of space
to the obliterating but unheard stellar roar,
and so to the dead-quiet edges of this universe
where starlight thins to blackness,
from the small circle of lamplight
on my desk.

Street with Porches

Not old as houses go
but nearing the limits of human longevity,
they were young when this century was new
in that tranquil interval
before its first great war
and wore their youthful candor
on front porches
adorned with flags on holidays,
and here and there a rocking chair
or bench swing.

Those who lived here
took refuge on their porches
from the summer heat
whiling away the evening hours
in a street-long common room
sharing their lives
like members of some vanished tribe.

Now, at century's end,
the porches are unattended
like belles past their prime
and we hunker down inside
with our devices,
hardly recognizing
those who live nearby.

Rain on a Country Road

Cars crawl along the blacktop
in aqueous gloom
like deep-sea creatures,
lights dangling
over their mouths.

Rain

tumbling, teeming, driving
rustling, rumbling, gurgling
tapping, pounding, thrumming, drumming
splattering, splashing, spraying
puddling, pooling, rushing.
Rain,
this hurricane.

Spider Webs

This morning I found
three spider webs
still wet with dew
embellishing the spruce behind our house,
their silken symmetry
shining against the dark trees
like silver-threaded crests
in a tapestry.

The Other Side of the Woods

There was a woods
near where we lived
when I was eight
that I often explored
without ever reaching the other side
forever distracted
by a clear brook
and its teeming tadpole populations,
green flashes of leaping frog,
elusive salamanders,
bird-crowded bowers,
furry creatures
glimpsed hurrying through the undergrowth,
large outcroppings of rock
(castles of the imagination),
raspberries ripening in late summer.

I fancied myself one of those woodsmen
I read about in my books
who ranged the vast forest
that once stretched
from the Atlantic to the Mississippi.
Years later
when I rounded the woods in a car
I found it was less than a mile across.

Central Park

Spread between palisades
of apartment blocks
like a lush valley between barren cliffs.
Instead of concrete canyons,
rustic vistas,
as if one had slipped
through a crevice in space.

In the Park

Idlers and lovers,
readers and sleepers,
clerks in blouses and skirts
or crisp shirts and creased trousers,
T-shirted workmen with long hair and tattoos,
ebullient sales girls,
bored matrons,
boys with ominous eyes,
sharp-eyed young men in expensive suits,
young mothers wheeling carriages
or with toddlers in tow,
dog walkers harnessed to their canines,
children engrossed in their play,
families in affectionate embrace,
equestrians and their mounts
in intimate symbiosis,
bikers, skaters, skate boarders, joggers,
all in appropriate apparel,
diverse ballplayers,
speakers of many tongues,
kite flyers and Frisbee flingers,
boaters, sunbathers, vendors,
pigeons and picnickers,
peace officers and perps,
house cats, squirrels, chipmunks,
ducks, geese, hawks, sparrows,
bees, ants, flies,
all crowd into the park.

The View from on High

quilted landscapes
of reassuring domesticity,
brute mountains,
spiky cities,
rivers, silver, serpentine,
bristling forests,
rice paddies
where mirrored sunlight flashes
through grids of green,
the tirelessly marching waves
of oceans and desert sands,
cloud castles' billowing towers,
patterns seen only
by birds
and airmen
and angels

The River

We don't often think
beside a small stream,
a brook we can straddle,
of the great river
in might become,
the ocean
into which it might empty,
flowing away clear
over its pebbled bed,
white flecked
down a perseverant slope,
over falls
through forests
gathering bulk and muscle
through farmlands
past towns
becoming broader
and darker,
past cities
that bridge and bind
yet cannot fully tame it,
then free
into the welcoming arms
of bay or estuary
and at last to the ocean,
like a son come back
from long wanderings.

Geometry

Another cloud shrouded winter morning.
Raindrops bead the windowpanes
refracting a dusky landscape
where streetlights still shine
enclosed in luminous spheres of rain
while at my desk
a cone of lamplight
pierces the enveloping darkness.

By the Plain of Jezreel

Once by the plain of Jezreel
across from the well of Gideon
where trumpets filled the night
across from Mount Gilboa
where Saul and his three sons died
I climbed a hill
and on the other side
saw hills ranging far and wide
over the Jordan and into the land beyond,
and heard voices in the wind.

Stormy Night

The lights are on in doorways
around the square,
warm saffron,
welcoming
amidst the ice-blue coruscations
of the storm.

Riverworld

Where the small midwestern river
issued from its lake
running smooth and brown
under a translucent vault of willows
I went exploring
when I was ten or so
imagining myself a voyageur
descending the mighty Mississippi.

There I encountered exotic fauna,
catfish with their mandarin whiskers,
looking learned and wise,
mud-puppies emerging from the water
like the first sea creatures
venturing onto land.

There sandy banks
sank into sepia waters
and a sunlit world
was steeped in mystery.

At the Beach

Summers at the beach
we turned pink on the yellow sand
wore grit like a second skin
fast high-stepped to the water
on sand sometimes so hot
we tried to run without touching ground,
splashed into the cooling water
tasting its brine
our nostrils full of that scent
that told us where we were
when we first drew near the shore,
swam out to waves
that carried us headlong on their crests
whirling us down as they crumbled
supplying us with breathless tales
when we were back on land.
Then we walked on the wet sand
where water followed in our footprints
while we gathered shells and sand dollars
and flat, smooth stones
rounded by the tireless work of water,
and watched white-vested gulls,
those dapper beachcombers,
waddle down the strand
or, balancing on a breeze,
glide down the shore
like notes of an arpeggio.

Then late in the day
when we were tired and the tide came in,
mesmerized by the ocean's pulse
we watched it rise on the beach,
dissolving sand castles,
so painstakingly wrought,
then, nonchalantly, slide back down,

and at night
the timeless sound of breaking waves
lulled us to sleep.

The Pond

There was a pond in my young years,
a place of reeds
reflected trees
and silky brown water
spilling over a weed-bearded dam,
a place where we swam from early spring
and skated in the early darkness of winter evenings,
a place of mysterious depths
where creatures vanished
into a green void
while tadpoles and minnows
swarmed on its verges
like exclamation points.

There I saw mallards, come down softly,
cruise, smoothly as pedal boats,
their broad feet massaging the water
until, sighting edibles,
they flipped forward,
to my delight,
as if on hinges.

There sometimes I surprised a frog,
hypnotized by my nearness,
stared into its knobby eyes
and saw its throat throb nervously.

There turtles sunned themselves
still as stones
while I waited, equally unmoving,
determined not to be the first to stir.

It was a small pond
but a world in my eyes.

Ode to an Island

My sister lives on a Caribbean isle,
little more than a dust mote on a map,
no realm of magic,
nor Ariel, nor Caliban
(though a touch of each),
no stage for grand drama,
merely the familiar theater of domesticity,

but birds flower there
and flowers take flight,
fish flash rainbows over the coral,
palm fronds sway to the wind
as if spellbound in dance,
and in the night
as you drift into sleep
you hear the waves upon the reef
intoning the ancient anthem of the sea.

In the Cloud Forest

Did you know there are cloud forests
where the trees are endlessly wrapped
in vaporous gauze
like the work of a publicity seeking artist,
or the puckish humor of a god,
where tree tops seem taller,
rising who knows how far,
up to the homes of giants perhaps,
and sounds ripple
through liquid air
eddying around the trees?
Those cries we hear—
what birds, what beasts?
Fusions of human and other parts?
What hideous creatures hide behind that fog?
Creatures of the mind, no doubt.

Streetlamps

A streetlamp shines through the leaves tonight
here in this suburb of my life,
another in front of a barracks in Verdun,
at a certain street corner in Heidelberg,
behind a row of chestnut trees on the Boulevard de
    Maillot
along a familiar stretch of sidewalk in New York,
sometimes with melancholy
sometimes with yearning
sometimes with the joy of life.

A streetlamp shines through the leaves tonight
and through the years.

Mountain Love

I fell in love with a mountain last night.
Not much of a mountain for height—
out west it would be just a hill—
but it stretches for a mysterious seventeen miles
behind our new home,
heavily wooded
sparsely inhabited
a terra incognita to be explored
like the woods behind our house when I was nine.

It's the only mountain for miles around
and I wondered how it got there
and why it has lasted so long.
I read that it's volcanic
but it's hard to imagine volcanoes here
in this land of farms and fields and rolling hills.
Then it's hard to imagine too
that this once might have been a loftier mountain.

I admire it for enduring
as one admires a ninety-year old.
It's wild I've been told
because its soil is impermeable and sour,
not good for houses or farms,
and I think it blessed.
Because it was scorned it lives free
untrammeled by those rows of immoderate houses
erupting across our countryside,
unshorn of its trees,
unkempt, acerbic, reclusive.
I love this old crone of a mountain.

Hills

There's something in me that loves a hill.
Perhaps it's that flatlands are flat,
two dimensional.
Yet plains can be stirring
marching from horizon to horizon
with unbroken stride.

Perhaps it's what's hidden by hills,
the mysteries in their folds,
unknown lands on the other side.

Perhaps it's a throwback to childhood,
seeing a good sledding slope,
or, games for older boys,
curves like those of women.

Perhaps it's that hills are less hospitable
to swarming humankind.

Whatever it is
my spirits rise
whenever I see a hill.

The Cemetery at the Top of Town

I took a walk this first day of spring
in the cemetery on the hill above our house,
one rich in the litter of history.
Dead from well over a century ago
lie in that ground.
Some of the marking stones,
washed by more than a hundred years of rain,
can no longer be read.

Veterans are buried there
of wars in the memory of some who live still
to those of their great-grandfathers.
Graves are there that hold the remains of men
who had been at Omaha Beach, perhaps,
Château-Thierry, San Juan Hill, Gettysburg.

Then there are the women who died young,
in their twenties and thirties,
veterans of those old wars of childbirth, I imagined.
And men in their fifties,
their hearts too strained by living?
A young man dead in 1918
perhaps in the great war
or the influenza epidemic of that year.
Infants too.
Then the couples who grew old together.

Most buried there were Catholic or Protestant
though I found an enclave of Russian Orthodox,
evidence of our melting pot,
and one couple with Jewish sounding names
holding hands as it were against the world
on that hill overlooking the town with its steeples
the deep valley beyond
and the hills on its far rim,
their woods and fields still covered with snow.

How many of these graves, I wondered, are visited
     still,
how many of their occupants remembered?
But not a bad place to be buried, I thought.
Though I don't hold with planting bodies in the
     ground,
at least those few who might care to stand over my
     bones
would have that view
of the town and the valley and the hills beyond
soon to be verdant with spring.

In the Cordillera

We pass a herd of alpacas
their coats powdered with snow.
Then the land falls away.
No telling how far or deep it goes
but beyond lies a high ridge
distant enough to be blue,
and beyond that a mountain,
its face all caked with snow,
so large it looms
as if the moon
had come down to pay a visit.

The Place Where the World Was Born

Upcountry once in Laos
I flew through a secluded valley
far from any road
where, amidst the deep green of paddies
and a scattering of houses raised on stilts,
a limestone column rose
like a lone skyscraper
a thousand feet up from the valley floor.
Surely this was the birth cord of the world.

Where Magic Dwells

Once in the Andes I visited a town
isolated in their eastern folds
where the mountains plunge into the Amazon.
We followed a dirt road rising three miles
then wound down a mile or more
from where a snow-capped mountain loomed
descending past tiers of terraces stepped by the
    Incas
perhaps a thousand years ago,
and there at the bottom
the town
with its church reminiscent of Spain
built centuries ago
by men from half a world away
who found this cranny
and stayed.
Today it's little changed,
one of those places
where magic still dwells.

Rievaulx Abbey

Once filled with glowing glass,
its tall arches
are full now with the green of fields and trees.
Sunlight plays in the empty nave,
the sky for a roof,
a shifting panorama,
Wedgwood blue with cameo clouds,
fretted by passing birds,
or dark but pierced with stars.
Wind, rain and snow freely flow
where worshippers once kneeled.
The altar is a knoll,
wild flowers the congregation.

Our Town

Sometimes on sunny days
we walk into town,
down a street
which above town is a country road
that crosses the mountain,
as it's called,
a wrinkle as mountains go,
but country as pure as you'll find in these parts.
From across the mountain the road comes
to its last ridge
where the town is laid out below
like a hobbyist's model,
punctuated by steeples.
Then the road cuts down
through wooded banks,
like those old English roads
worn into the ground,
by centuries of wheels,
past the cemetery
with its grave chronology.

Descending farther,
the road, now called an Avenue,
surges up a little hill
that launches it over the railroad tracks
then down the other side,
past the old, Charles Adams station,
and an ice cream parlor,
open only in the warm months,
past rows of tall oaks and maples
and houses built some hundred years ago
when the railroad came to town,
the houses of merchants and bankers,
doctors and lawyers,
with turrets and bays

and wraparound porches,
and so on down to main street.
Broad Street it's called,
and broad it is
as one on an Our Town movie set.
It reaches east
to a place where Washington slept,
and had his headquarters.
John Hart from our town
signed the Declaration of Independence,
then hid from the king's men
in the crannies of the mountain,
leaving his name to the street on which we live,
then a country road
that ran past his farm.
At the Historical Society
you can find
yellowing pictures of the farm
looking like Currier & Ives.

West past hills and woods and fields and farms,
there's a town on the Delaware,
where the river, though far from its mouth, is
    already broad.
There great sturgeon once surged through clear
    water,
till the colonists came and fished them out.
It was a workingmen's town
till the gentry came
and bought them out.
Now it's restaurants, galleries, antique shops
and bric-a-brac galore.

Back on Broad Street
going out the Delaware way
we pass the pharmacy,
part of no chain,

a restaurant,
old houses from pre-railroad days,
a beauty shop, a gallery,
antique shops—they've colonized us too—
and a café,
or, if we go the other way
a clapboard church, its rectory,
an enormous beech,
already tall when the railroad came,
the library, all in old brick,
and a bait shop.

That's almost half the center of town
and better than half of heaven

Our Piece of Country

Our small piece of the planet,
the country around our town,
is nothing much compared to mountains,
deep forests or broad rivers.
Its hills are gentle,
its woods modest,
its streams unobtrusive,
but its curves are sensual,
it's verdant,
and it's ours.

Moonlight on Snow

The night is lighter for snow,
roofs and fields phosphorescent,
the moon's pearly light
etching a filigree
of leafless trees,
on the nacreous ground.

Pemaquid Point

You feel the force of the ocean here,
the wind driven waves
pounding the water white,
fraying the land's rocky edges,
even holding the season back,
the leaves still small and pale here,
now in this middle of May.

You feel the water's weight and breadth,
filling the deep Atlantic basin,
stretching to far-away continents
under many-hued skies.

Our Backyard

Reading something rural
by a poet from Vermont
I think to myself it would be nice
to live in such a place,
explore it with my poetry,
but then I look out our back window and see
a sky of very blue and white
a trio of goldfinches at our feeder
a squad of robins
combing the yard for worms,
and a young squirrel
chasing a robin playfully.

Fog on a July Morning

Pre-dawn fog
veils the trees
blurs hard lines
dissolves solidity.
Houses loom like ships.
Our familiar town
becomes a mystery.

Paleontology

Trolleys may be long gone
but on some streets
you can still see their rails
poking through the pavement
like bones.

Fog on the Eastern Seaboard

It's foggy this morning
not just here
nor in the nearby deep valley
where mist often gathers,
but all the way into town,
my headlights beating like moths
against the whiteness.
On the radio they're reporting
fog in Central Park
sixty miles north
and I picture a long low cloud
stretching that distance,
a vaporous giant
slumbering.

Fête Champêtre

I open a window shade and find
a yard full of birds and butterflies,
robins bobbing for worms,
mourning doves davening for seed,
goldfinches upside down at their feeder
sparrows spearing what falls,
tigers in force on the butterfly bush,
a black swallowtail on a coneflower,
cabbage whites everywhere.
It's as crowded as Times Square.

Calendar Art

From the mountain,
looking down,
this New England town
looks like a tabletop model
with its white church steeple,
the river embracing it,
and the hills beyond
veiled now in spring chartreuse,
or later garbed in summer green,
gaudy with fall colors
or in winter's white gown
embroidered with leafless trees.

The Lake

There was a lake in Michigan
where I spent my childhood summers,
a glacial lake
with hilly banks
scooped out of flat farmland.
A mile wide and three long,
it was big enough
for the far shore to seem a foreign place,
adding to the mystery of the water
with its large carp that hovered in the shallows like
    blimps
and its murky depths,
tall seaweed reaching up at you
as you swam into the deep water
where there were primitive slashing carnivores
alligator gar
rumored to have once attacked a man.

But there were also the sunfish and bluegills,
their rainbow hues visible in the shallows,
bass, streamlined and speckled,
minnows that would swarm away from you
flashing out of the water in formation,
and boats,
sailboats with their canvas wings,
small motorboats
their back-mounted motors buzzing
like insects of legendary decibels,
and the big ones with their inboard engines,
the Cadillacs of that watery place
emerging from their houses with a self-satisfied
    rumble
to turn and breast the water,
cleaving it,
filling the air with spray,
rocking smaller boats with their waves.

Then there was the Honeymoon
a two-decker
miniature version of the larger craft
that plied the far vaster waters of Lake Michigan.
It made the rounds of the lake on weekends
tooting its train-like whistle
and announcing over a loudspeaker
"Around the lake and down the river to Watervliet
on the Honeymoon."
Every weekend the Honeymoon,
regular as church bells.
The boat has no doubt long since been scrapped
but it still makes the rounds of the lake in my
    memory,
its ghostly speaker calling us in its wake.

Dunes

When I was a boy, I often visited
the dunes along the Lake Michigan shore,
hills of sand taller than trees
half covered with tenacious grass and pines
but opening on the water side
like puddings
their insides spilling out in long sandy slopes
down which you could run and slide
with avalanche abandon
and come up clean,
nothing more than sand in your clothes
and laughter in your mind.

Once on the Prairie

Once when I was young
I drove north on the prairie
very early one summer morning,
the sun just rising
and rolling back before it
a thick blanket of fog,
revealing houses and cornfields
woods and free-standing trees,
mostly tall elms
shaped like acacia or Roman pines
though at the time
I didn't know those trees
or their continents,
but the fog,
taller than any tree,
rolling back so gradually,
like a reverse, slow motion tsunami,
was enormous enough to awe me
without any learnèd allusions.

Fences

Good fences may or may not make good neighbors
but they make their mark on the landscape,
some mimicking nature's harmonious lines,
others a blemish on Earth's designs.
Some can be crossed
with an easy climb,
others just say Keep Out.
Some sing of the works of hands,
hedgerows and windrows planted
in green and pleasant lands,
stones from glacial fields
piled in laborious lines,
split rails displaying their hearts of wood,
but others, down to their chainlink names,
mutter of dark Satanic mills.

Overture

The day grows light behind a scrim of haze.
A veiled sun takes the stage.
The hills across the valley still in shadow,
the river shines, serpentine,
spotlit by the sun's first rays.
Enter townsmen
going to their trades.
The music swells.

The Names of Mountains

The Andes, where I've lived and worked
among the snow-capped peaks of Ecuador
with their resonant names,
Chimborazo, Antisana, Sangay,
the nevados of Bolivia
looming over the impossible blue of Titicaca,
the Adirondacks seen from across Lake Champlain
the whole range on display
like a model on a tabletop,
or the gentle Catskills,
a place where a man could sleep for twenty years,
the Hindu Kush
with its Shangri-La valleys
and a soaring mountain
named Tirich Mir
as if it were a warlord or a conqueror or a god,
and others I haven't seen
except in pictures,
the Carpathians, the Balkans, the Caucasus,
the Urals, the Altai,
the Tien Shan,
the Himalayas, the Karakoram,
the names of mountains spoken with love and awe.

The Valley and the Hills

Our house overlooks a broad valley
spread out in miniature,
church steeples smaller than spindles,
houses and barns like children's toys,
farm fields, woods and roads
patches of river
calmly reflecting the sky.
If you watch patiently
you might even see a boat
or a grazing deer
small as fine print.

And in the distance
a long line of hills,
mostly a blue-grayness,
streaked sometimes with sunlight,
hiding secrets in their folds,
wolves, mountain lions, perhaps,
fauns, unicorns,
bears at least, coyotes, wolverines,
clearings, springs, streams, ravines,
places where the imagination can run free
seeking magic, wild things.

Lakes I've Known

It wasn't Como or Wannsee
Geneva or Tahoe
Atitlan or Titicaca
but it was mine,
the lake where I spent my childhood summers,
occupying a space in my memory
larger than its square miles.
Paw Paw it was called,
humble as a teepee,
but the lake where I learned my way in the water
swam and sailed, rowed and fished.

Then there was Lake Michigan.
I once lived just yards from it,
saw it in all seasons
even with ice piling up on the shore
as if it were trying to climb from its basin.

And the lake in northern Minnesota
where my uncle took me fishing when I was 15…
I don't remember its name
but I do remember the screaming loon laughter
I first heard there.
And the chain of remote lakes in Canada
where I went with my uncle the next summer.
No houses in sight
just moose grazing in the shallows
and Cree gathering wild rice.

Oh I've been to Lac Leman
Titicaca, Atitlan,
Tahoe, Malawi, the Tonle Sap.
So much beauty,
but not mine.

Sidereal Navigation

At night
after the lights in our house are out
the LED's display like embers,
like glowworms in a river bank.
Though they're not bright enough
to light my path
I can navigate by them,
as if by the stars.

County Fair

The fair has come to town
as it does this time every year,
summer fading,
foreshadowings of fall in the air,
a still hot day,
an extra-blue sky,
clouds piled high as wedding cakes.

On the fairground:
booths and rides that sprang up overnight
and will vanish just as suddenly;
cotton candy, corn dogs, pulled pork,
funnel cakes, fried dough, fried everything,
fifty-star American cuisine;
a tattoo parlor, a tarot reader,
game booths—odds favor the house—
rides with animal-shaped pods
for children to ride like joeys,
a Ferris wheel towering over all,
chairman of the rotary.

Pig races out of Tampa
just after the Republican convention there.
A man with menacing reptiles,
Kachunga and the Alligator Show.
I'm reminded of a half-blind man
I saw once in a park
displaying trained birds in a cage.
The birds sang
for coins dropped
by too few passersby.

Where Men Once Dwelled

There's a graveyard in the woods
high on a ridge in Lagrangeville
a town in upstate New York
that's as small as its name suggests.
The graveyard too is small
eight or ten graves perhaps.
There's not much other sign of civilization
in those woods,
merely a houseless foundation
and the sparse remnants of fieldstone walls
to tell you there were once farms and families
    there.
But the land was hilly
and those who farmed it
went west to where the land was flat
and enriched by the floods of broad rivers
and the communities that once thrived in these
    eastern hills
expired, leaving only a few listing slabs of stone
and tumbling walls
hidden in the woods.

A Glimpse of River

From our house on the hill
we can see a bit of the river
a mile or so away,
just a pond-like segment,
and it seldom crosses my mind
that we live near a great river,
stretching four hundred miles
from source to sea
like an offspring of the mythical serpent
that was said to girdle the Earth.

There's Something about a Bridge

bearing us over rivers, gorges,
lofting us over water and air,
taking us places
we'd otherwise be unlikely to go,

the graceful curve of arches,
honeycombed steel beams,
webs of cable,

there's something about a bridge
that carries us high and away.

I Live Down by the River

It's winter now
and amidst the ice flows
I watch the buffleheads and mergansers
diving for their food
the way boys used to dive
for coins thrown by cruise ship passengers.

In spring it's the ducklings and goslings
looking too fuzzy to float
but sailing securely in line behind their parents,

in summer sailboats
winging their birdlike way
across the river, here where it's miles wide,

in fall migrant swans
and geese, honking raucously,

and all year long gulls
in acrobatic flight,
boats and ships of various shapes and sizes
and the big sky—
Montana you're not the only place—
with its clouds and colors,
the shape and hue of fantasy,
sunrises and sunsets,
big moons rising,
moons full and crescent, half and gibbous,
stars and planets,
and rainbows arcing panoramically
over the far bank.

I live down by the river
where the river lives near me.

After the Rain

the sky is clear and clean,
blue as wedgwood,
clouds cameoed,
porcelain the high half-moon.

Clouds

Over the high ridge
clouds blossom
from an emptiness
of flame-blue sky,
blossom and vanish
and blossom and vanish again
in a display
of planetary
prestidigitation.

The Night Is an Ocean

Clouds float
on its phosphorescent waters
like ghostly islands
while on the nocturnal shore
a crescent moon,
entangled in leafless trees,
waits for a tide to lift it free.

Clouds Gather

In all the wide sky
there were only
a few small clouds
like sheep scattered
across a vast meadow,
until the hounds of heaven came
herding them into rain.

Balloon Fair

A skyful of balloons
hanging on mere heated air
wafting us back to a time
when sedate spheres
grazed in blue meadows
and man rose above the earth
suspended from silent globes,
when the atmosphere was disturbed
only by the subtle cries of birds.

The Kite

dances on air
still joined to our hand
capering to our command
its string an extension
of our nerves.
Through it we reach
cloud high
as if we rode the wind
and the whole wide sky
blew through our hair.

Rowing at Evening

I like to row in evening
when dark trees
frame the still lake
and the water mirrors the sky,
to glide over the smooth surface,
stroking in slow rhythm
leaning back on the oars,
sending spirals spinning
like galaxies
into the reflected sky.

Sidereal Dissatisfaction

One day
I'd like to see the Milky Way again.
I saw it often in my youth,
and was impressed
but didn't think about it much.
Now I see only a few stars
sifting through a shroud of light
a burka we've donned willingly.
The stars may seem multitudinous
to you who were born
in recent years,
but many of you
have never seen the Milky Way.

My First Shooting Star

I don't remember when it was
that I first saw a shooting star
but I can feel the excitement still
of seeing one suddenly
streak across the sky.
I don't think I knew
how large stars are
nor the difference between a meteor and a star,
but I remember still the thrill I felt
seeing one
break ranks and race across the sky.

Empress Moon

The moon
with her porcelain complexion
reigns over the night sky,
her realm of dark matter.
The lightless flame of the cypress trees
and the spiky limbs of leafless trees
reach skyward
obeisantly.

Just Before Dawn

Pale green seeps
into the soft fabric of the night
as if dipped in light.
No stars in view;
their glitter subdued
by dawn's tide
and the moon's faint luminescence.
Only an appliqué of trees
adorns this dark tapestry.
That and a crescent moon.

December Afternoon

a wafer of moon
in late afternoon
and a dusting of sunlight
on a roof across the way,
the goddess of night
and the god of day
in rare cohabitation

Floating World

The moon,
like a Japanese lantern,
hangs from the branches of a leafless tree
on a screen of deep blue sky,
as if a print by Hokusai.

Fanfare for a Setting Sun

It rained all day
but just before sunset
the sun shone through a gap in the clouds
a huge sphere of fire
balanced on the horizon.
"It may be clearing" I said
but the gap closed
before the sun went down
and my wife delivered her rejoinder:
"The sun set without fanfare",
as if sunsets had a soundtrack.
A splendid idea I thought,
something by Beethoven perhaps.

That's Amore

The moon can be seen
from our front window
rising this very moment
from the hilltops across the valley.
We see it so only this time of year
when the leaves are gone
and our satellite is in the right quarter.
It's full tonight, a perfect disk, for our delectation,
yellow as can be,
looking like one of those big cheese wheels
you used to see
hanging from the ceilings
of Italian delicatessens.

Lamb-white Days

It was fine today,
this fifteenth of May,
flocks of fleecy clouds
grazing in cornflower fields
watered by yesterday's rain.

Montgolfier Returns

When I opened the shades this morning
there was a large balloon
outside our window,
one of those of man-bearing size,
ribbed and gondolaed and gaily colored
like something from a Jules Verne story.
It was drifting slowly toward us
growing larger as it came,
drifting slowly
into the 21st century.

Floodlight

Sunlight spills over the horizon
bathing the facades across the courtyard in tepid
    light,
pours into our kitchen
cascading over the jade plant
by the window ledge,
collects in pools on the floor,
then overflows
flooding the house with brightness.

The Shores of Morning

I was up before dawn this morning
as first light
infused the dark waters of night
dissolving the stars,
save for Venus
which still flared
in the dusky sky.
Then the sun came
flooding the shores of morning
with molten light.

The Dance of Morning

Morning mist veils the trees
turning their plain raiment of leaves
into a diaphanous gown
threaded with sunlight.

Then a breeze stirs the trees
and birds begin to chatter
like tambourines.

Homage to Omar Khayyam

Just before dawn
a crescent moon and Jupiter
shine in the boundless clarity
of a December sky
like a flag unfurled
over the ramparts
of morning.

Renewal

Luster streaks
the dawn sky
reminding me
of waiting for deer
at the edge of a woods
in the brittle cold
of a December morning,
or marching out,
a young soldier,
under bright banners of cloud
as day dawned over the pine barrens,
of being early on the road,
full of the exhilaration
of driving away
from everyday demands,
or of coming home
after a night on the town
fatigue dispelled
by that elixir of early morning.

How Many Dawns?

How many dawns have I seen,
the stars wink out,
the horizon bronze with light,
pale blue suffuse the blackness of the night,
the sun's fierce phoenix rise from Earth's edge?
Too few.
So few I could easily have kept count.

What did men do before we had clocks
and nine to five?
Did they rise with the dawn
or sleep while the world grew light?
Once we had roosters to roust us out,
but you'd be hard put to find a rooster hereabouts
in our suburban world
or amidst the cities' crowded towers.

So we pass much of our lives
waking to washed out skies
and seldom witness
dawn's shining hours.

After the Storm

After a day of sleet and slush,
skies of gloomy gray
and a nightlong drumroll of rain,
morning comes
sounding a note of sunlight
on the slope across the valley
while in the eastern sky
chords of blue and gold strike up
an overture to a new day.

Rainy Evening Near the Hudson
Homage to Childe Hassam

Rain runs black on the street
down to the river
through a fringe of trees.

On the far bank
lights glitter
on the gray of evening
twined in the branches and leaves,
and lamps send yellow streamers
up the pavement.

Rain in the City

I

Rain threads
from a darkened sky
weaving soft patterns
with the gray light,
spreading its mantle
on the city's tall shoulders.

II

Wind ruffles the pools
of yesterday's rain
splintering the reflected city
with a cubist hand.

The Bridge

It was a city like others of its time,
of low buildings
and slender steeples,
until, in its third century,
two towers of stone were raised.
Higher than any cathedral,
they could be seen
from every part of the city, and beyond,
soaring above all other works of men,
not to strive toward heaven
or flatter a capricious king
but to span a channel
between two arms of the sea.
Longer it was than any bridge before
and loftier
so that tall-masted ships
could glide beneath
as easily as gulls.
For this it was hung from cables
woven against the sky
like a web wide as a forest
in which to catch the stars.

Sidewalks

Sidewalks are where we walked,
toddled, sauntered, strided,
ambled, strutted, strolled
rode our baby buggies,
skated, biked,
stood around with our hands in our pockets
wisecracking,
watching the girls go by,
learned to smoke,
practiced yo-yo,
and peripatetic philosophy,
watched TV in store windows,
lined up for the movies,
bought newspapers, frankfurters, pretzels, books,
ate anything we could hold in one hand,
waited for dates,
walked hand in hand,
walked our dogs,
put out the trash,
heard clattering garbage cans,
steel drum bands
and schizoid ravings,
gave money to panhandlers
or pretended not to see or hear,
in the city
where our youth was spent.

Forsaken City

Passing this small city at sunrise
I see it sleeping fitfully by its river
where once working mills lie idle
windows broken
smokestacks still.
Here as dawn breaks
I imagine hundreds
turning over in their beds
pulling the covers up,
nowhere to go today
or any day.
Yet the salmon sun
still swims up its ladder of clouds
and flights of geese slide overhead
as if this place were forest still
instead of a city turned to rust.

New York of the Mind

When I think of Manhattan
I see it on a fine fall or spring day,
not in summer heat nor winter cold.
I see it in brilliant sunlight,
trimmed with half leafless or budding trees,
not in winter's piercing light
nor summer haze.
I can picture it in other times of the year
but if I let my mind run free
I see a New York good for sauntering
in youth's tender seasons.

As I Remember Jerusalem

The old city
its narrow streets
fit for no more than men on foot,
donkeys and their carts,
streets paved with stones
that knew the feet
of David perhaps,
prophets, Jeshua and his apostles
men of imperial Rome
the armies of young Islam
crusaders out of the west
(Provence, Chaumont,
where cedars of Lebanon still grow,
Tuscany, Sussex, the Palatinate),
streets given over to tourists now,
merchandise hanging in passageways
like laundry from tenements,
houses of pale Jerusalem stone,
the cliff-like wall of the temple mount
where the sanctuary stood
two thousand years ago,
edifices from Roman times
excavated but still underground
like impacted teeth,
testimony that the city has piled up,
a rubbish heap.

I scarcely remember the modern city
the new buildings
the wide streets,
just the old,
memorial,
battleground.

Fog

it's scrim softening
the world's hard edges,
turning wakefulness to dream,
the city's clamor to lullaby.

www.ingramcontent.com/pod-product-compliance
Lightning Source LLC
LaVergne TN
LVHW051419080426
835508LV00022B/3165